A CENTURY OF
LIVERPOOL

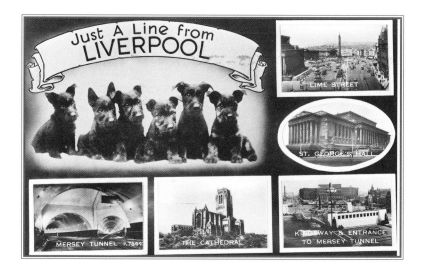

St George's Hall, Liverpool, early in the twentieth century.

A CENTURY OF LIVERPOOL

CLIFF HAYES

SUTTON PUBLISHING

First published in 1999 by Sutton Publishing Limited

This new paperback edition first published in 2007 by
Sutton Publishing, an imprint of NPI Media Group
Cirencester Road · Chalford · Stroud · Gloucestershire · GL6 8PE

British Library Cataloguing in Publication Data
A catalogue record for this book is available from the British Library.

ISBN 978-0-7509-4906-4

Front endpaper: Bold Street, Liverpool, *c.* 1900.
Back endpaper: The *QEII* graces the River Mersey.
Half title page: A postcard from Liverpool, *c.* 1938.
Title page: Lord Street, *c.* 1909.

Compiled with the co-operation of
the *Liverpool Daily Post* and the *Liverpool Echo*

Typeset in Photina.
Typesetting and origination by
Sutton Publishing.
Printed and bound in England.

Contents

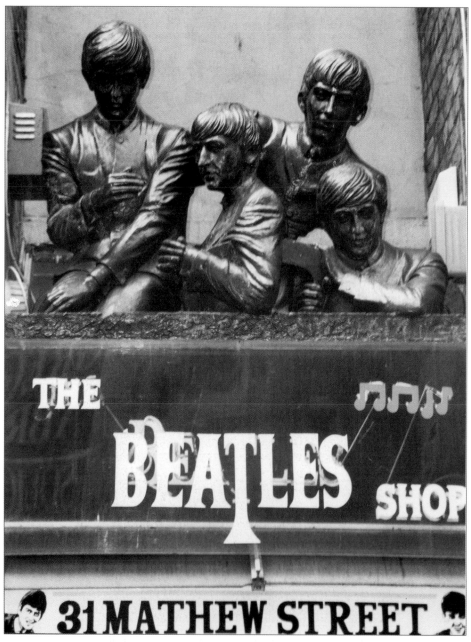

This bronze half-statue of the Fab Four graces the entrance to the Beatles shop. Sculpted by David Hughes its official title is 'From Us to You'. It was funded by Beatles fans from all over the world. Put up in 1984 it was the first Beatles statue anywhere.

Britain: A Century of Change

Churchill in RAF uniform giving his famous victory sign, 1948.
(Illustrated London News)

The sixty years ending in 1900 were a period of huge transformation for Britain. Railway stations, post-and-telegraph offices, police and fire stations, gasworks and gasometers, new livestock markets and covered markets, schools, churches, football grounds, hospitals and asylums, water pumping stations and sewerage plants totally altered the urban scene, and the country's population tripled with more than seven out of ten people being born in or moving to the towns. The century that followed, leading up to the Millennium's end in 2000, was to be a period of even greater change.

When Queen Victoria died in 1901, she was measured for her coffin by her grandson Kaiser Wilhelm, the London prostitutes put on black mourning and the blinds came down in the villas and terraces spreading out from the old town centres. These centres were reachable by train and tram, by the new bicycles and still newer motor cars, were connected by the new telephone, and lit by gas or even electricity. The shops may have been full of British-made cotton and woollen clothing but the grocers and butchers were selling cheap Danish bacon, Argentinian beef, Australasian mutton and tinned or dried fish and fruit from Canada, California and South Africa. Most of these goods were carried in British-built-and-crewed ships burning Welsh steam coal.

King Edward VII receiving 'addresses of welcome' at the Guildhall, Gloucester, June 1909. *(Sutton collection)*

As the first decade moved on, the Open Spaces Act meant more parks, bowling greens and cricket pitches. The First World War transformed the place of women, as they took over many men's jobs. Its other legacies were the war memorials which joined the statues of Victorian worthies in main squares round the land. After 1918 death duties and higher taxation bit hard, and a quarter of England changed hands in the space of only a few years.

The multiple shop – the chain store – appeared in the high street: Marks & Spencer, Sainsburys, Maypole, Lipton's, Home & Colonial, the Fifty Shilling Tailor, Burton, Boots, W.H. Smith. The shopper was spoilt for choice, attracted by the brash fascias and advertising hoardings for national brands like Bovril, Pears Soap, and Ovaltine. Many new buildings began to be seen, such as garages, motor showrooms, picture palaces (cinemas), 'palais de dance', and ribbons of 'semis' stretched along the roads and new bypasses and onto the new estates nudging the green belts.

During the 1920s cars became more reliable and sophisticated as well as commonplace, with developments like the electric self-starter making them easier for women to drive. Who wanted to turn a crank handle in the new short skirt? This was, indeed, the electric age as much as the

Crowds celebrate Armistice Day outside Buckingham Palace as the royal family appears on the balcony, 1918. (*Illustrated London News*)

9

motor era. Trolley buses, electric trams and trains extended mass transport and electric light replaced gas in the street and the home, which itself was groomed by the vacuum cleaner.

A major jolt to the march onward and upward was administered by the Great Depression of the early 1930s. The older British industries – textiles, shipbuilding, iron, steel, coal – were already under pressure from foreign competition when this worldwide slump arrived. Luckily there were new diversions to alleviate the misery. The 'talkies' arrived in the cinemas; more and more radios and gramophones were to be found in people's homes; there were new women's magazines, with fashion, cookery tips and problem pages; football pools; the flying feats of women pilots like Amy Johnson; the Loch Ness Monster; cheap chocolate and the drama of Edward VIII's abdication.

Houghton of Aston Villa beats goalkeeper Crawford of Blackburn to score the second of four goals, 1930s. *(Illustrated London News)*

Things were looking up again by 1936 and new light industry was booming in the Home Counties as factories struggled to keep up with the demand for radios, radiograms, cars and electronic goods, including the first television sets. The threat from Hitler's Germany meant rearmament, particularly of the airforce, which stimulated aircraft and aero engine firms. If you were lucky and lived in the south, there was good money to be earned. A semi-detached house cost £450, a Morris Cowley £150. People may have smoked like chimneys but life expectancy, since 1918, was up by 15 years while the birth rate had almost halved.

In some ways it is the little memories that seem to linger longest from the Second World War: the kerbs painted white to show up in the blackout, the rattle of ack-ack shrapnel on roof tiles, sparrows killed by bomb blast. The biggest damage, apart from London, was in the south-west (Plymouth, Bristol) and the Midlands (Coventry, Birmingham). Postwar reconstruction was rooted in the Beveridge Report which set out the expectations for the Welfare State. This, together with the nationalisation of the Bank of England, coal, gas, electricity and the railways, formed the programme of the Labour government in 1945.

WAAF personnel tracing the movement of flying bombs and Allied fighters on a plotting table, 1944. *(Illustrated London News)*

British soldiers taking part
in an anti-gas drill, 1939.
(*Illustrated London News*)

Times were hard in the late 1940s, with rationing even more
stringent than during the war. Yet this was, as has been said, 'an
innocent and well-behaved era'. The first let-up came in 1951 with
the Festival of Britain and there was another fillip in 1953 from the
Coronation, which incidentally gave a huge boost to the spread of TV.
By 1954 leisure motoring had been resumed but the Comet – Britain's
best hope for taking on the American aviation industry – suffered a series

11

of mysterious crashes. The Suez debacle of 1956 was followed by an acceleration in the withdrawal from Empire, which had begun in 1947 with the Independence of India. Consumerism was truly born with the advent of commercial TV and most homes soon boasted washing machines, fridges, electric irons and fires.

A police radio controller at Scotland Yard, 1947. *(Illustrated London News)*

The *Lady Chatterley* obscenity trial in 1960 was something of a straw in the wind for what was to follow in that decade. A collective loss of inhibition seemed to sweep the land, as the Beatles and the Rolling Stones transformed popular music, and retailing, cinema and the theatre were revolutionised. Designers, hairdressers, photo-graphers and models moved into places vacated by an Establishment put to flight by the new breed of satirists spawned by *Beyond the Fringe* and *Private Eye*.

In the 1970s Britain seems to have suffered a prolonged hangover after the excesses of the previous decade. Ulster, inflation and union troubles were not made up for by entry into the EEC, North Sea Oil, Women's Lib or, indeed, Punk Rock. Mrs Thatcher applied the corrective in the 1980s, as the country moved over more and more from its old manufacturing base to providing services, consulting, advertising, and expertise in the 'invisible' market of high finance or in IT.

The post-1945 townscape has seen changes to match those in the worlds of work, entertainment and politics. In 1952 the Clean Air Act served notice on smogs and pea-souper fogs, smuts and blackened buildings, forcing people to stop burning coal and go over to smokeless sources of heat and energy. In the same decade some of the best urban building took place in the 'new towns' like Basildon, Crawley, Stevenage and Harlow. Elsewhere open warfare was declared on slums and what was labelled inadequate, cramped, back-to-back, two-up, two-down, housing. The new 'machine for living in' was a flat in a high-rise block. The architects and planners who promoted these were in league with the traffic engineers, determined to keep the motor car moving whatever the price in multi-storey car parks, meters, traffic wardens and ring roads. The old pollutant, coal smoke, was replaced by petrol and diesel exhaust, and traffic noise.

Fast food was no longer only a pork pie in a pub or fish-and-chips. There were Indian curry houses, Chinese take-aways and American-style hamburgers, while the drinker could get away from beer in a wine bar. Under the impact of television the big Gaumonts and Odeons closed or were rebuilt as multi-screen cinemas, while the palais de dance gave way to discos and clubs.

From the late 1960s the introduction of listed buildings and conservation areas, together with the growth of preservation societies, put a brake on 'comprehensive redevelopment'. The end of the century and the start of the Third Millennium saw new challenges to the health of towns and the wellbeing of the nine out of ten people who now live urban lives. The fight is on to prevent town centres from dying, as patterns of housing and shopping change, and edge-of-town supermarkets exercise the attractions of one-stop shopping. But as banks and department stores close, following the haberdashers, greengrocers, butchers and ironmongers, there are signs of new growth such as farmers' markets, and corner stores acting as pick-up points where customers collect shopping ordered on-line from web sites.

Futurologists tell us that we are in stage two of the consumer revolution: a shift from mass consumption to mass customisation driven by a desire to have things that fit us and our particular lifestyle exactly, and for better service. This must offer hope for small city-centre shop premises, as must the continued attraction of physical shopping, browsing and being part of a crowd: in a word, 'shoppertainment'. Another hopeful trend for towns is the growth in the number of young people postponing marriage and looking to live independently, alone, where there is a buzz, in 'swinging single cities'. Theirs is a 'flats-and-

13

Manchester during the Commonwealth Games in 2002. The city, like others all over the country, has experienced massive redevelopment and rejuvenation in recent years. (*Chris Makepeace*)

cafés' lifestyle, in contrast to the 'family suburbs', and certainly fits in with government's aim of building 60 per cent of the huge amount of new housing needed on 'brown' sites, recycled urban land. There looks to be plenty of life in the British town yet.

Liverpool: An Introduction

Liverpool in 1900 was an exciting place to be. Plans were in place for a new Waterfront, the old Pier Head Docks were going and trade with the British Empire was steady. Queen Victoria was still on the throne, and Victoria liked Liverpool. She may have been past her best, and not seen in public much, but she was never slow in granting royal patronage to anything connected with England's second city. The council celebrations to welcome her in 1900 were somewhat muted by the age and health of Queen Victoria; nobody wanted to plan a great feast only to have it cancelled if the Queen became very ill, or even died on the eve of the celebrations. As it turned out she lived 12 months into the new century.

The challenge from Manchester over the Ship Canal had been strong, and Liverpool did not come out of the contest well. Shipping was still increasing and steam power now had a grip of the liners sailing in and out of the port. Cruising was becoming more popular. It provided just what the upper class and monied people wanted: 'A holiday in the sun, without the problems of foreign travel.' With its rail links to every part of the country Liverpool became one of the main ports for cruise liners. This meant that vast numbers of people passed through the port every day, and Liverpool provided the services that the wealthy cruise passengers required, such as fine hotels, excellent transport to and from their ship, and shops to rival any in the world selling the latest fashions.

Liverpool was the first city in the world to have a medical officer and his team were slowly but surely clearing away the slums and cellar dwellings that had blighted life in the city during the mid-1800s. It wasn't going to be an overnight miracle, but the city was really tackling the problems.

Liverpool is almost unique among British cities in that it owes its very existence to the fact that it is on the coast. It flourished because the River Mersey and 'the Pool' gave good shelter to shipping, and it acquired prominence because of the ships, shipping companies and 'King Cotton'. Only Bristol has a merchant naval history to match Liverpool's.

The Merchant Navy Memorial at the Pier Head.

POLICE BATON CHARGE
LPOOL STRIKE 1911   No 13

In the history books 1911 went down as the year the Riot Act was read in Liverpool, but only 50 years before that factory and mill owners cut wages, laid people off and even closed workplaces just to keep their profits up.

As the century progressed a feeling of equality gripped the people of the north. Liverpool suffered many strikes and unrest in the years prior to 'the Great War', and that unrest surfaced again in the mid-1920s and the early 1930s. Blame can be apportioned to both sides, workers and management, over the century, and we see the balance of power swinging from one party to the other, especially in the 1950s and '60s when a strike was a strike and nobody and nothing moved, without union say-so.

The First World War ended much of the bickering as Great Britain turned to face an even bigger threat, and made a unified effort against 'the Hun'. Every town and city in the north-west gave men for their 'Pals' regiments, and conscripts into the Royal Navy. Liverpool had to give more – the thousands of men that made up the Merchant Navy, and not many people realise just how high the losses at sea were.

This book has been crafted, built, honed and shaped to follow the fortunes of Liverpool right through the twentieth century. I hope that you let it lead you, decade by decade, up to the milestone of a new

Dockers went on strike in 1911 and the unrest quickly spread. Here we see a very rare photograph of police charging. The troubles reached a peak in August 1911 when two men were shot dead by soldiers and hundreds were hurt battling with the police.

century and millennium that marks the end of the book. Liverpool is always a busy place and I've tried to make the book a busy place as well, including all the rebuilding of the 1930s, and exciting projects, like the Mersey Tunnel, that brought so much change. I feel this is a good book, an informative and interesting book and I hope you agree.

The May Day Parade passing Bunney's Corner, *c.* 1933. (See also p. 53)

Liverpool gets an unfair press from certain sections of the media, and though we say 'Words can never hurt us', they do: they slow outside investment, they put off those who don't know the city and the kind, friendly, big-hearted people who outweigh 100 to 1 those whose deeds bring bad publicity. Mind you, sense of humour or not, Liverpool, council and all, has a habit of shooting itself in the foot, just when things seem to be going well.

I've enjoyed putting this offering together and hope you get the same feeling of enjoyment when reading it.

May the twenty-first century be good and kind to you and yours.

Cliff Hayes

Welcome to the Twentieth Century

The corner of Old Haymarket and Great Charlotte Street at the start of the century.
Waiters and customers pose obligingly.

The rise of Liverpool from King John's Charter in 1207 was slow but steady. The fact that the city had a military significance in sending troops and armaments abroad led to the construction of Liverpool Castle. The slave trade had come and thankfully gone by the turn of the twentieth century, and Liverpool's prosperity in 1900 was based on imports and exports of cotton, timber and people.

A look at Liverpool as it was before the twentieth century had begun. Above we see a drawing of the docks around 1860; on the right, we see the front at Liverpool; below, a scene at the waterfront from the same era.

Liverpool traders thought of themselves as 'gentlemen' and built themselves 'gentlemen's residences' in the centre of town.

Again 1860 and a Herdman drawing of the view looking down Church Street towards the river.

This is Lime Street as it appeared just before the railways arrived.

21

Castle Street, looking towards the Town Hall. *c.* 1912. The street took its name from the castle that once stood here on high ground dominating the river. On the top of the Town Hall sits a statue of Minerva (the Roman Goddess of Wisdom – an appropriate place for her to be). There is another school of thought that believes the figure is Britannia.

Opposite, top: Lime Street at the start of the twentieth century. St George's Hall stands proudly to the left of the picture, while the London North Western Railway Hotel dominates the right.

Opposite, bottom: One of the earliest picture postcards of Liverpool showing a view looking up Bold Street. *c.* 1904. Note the Mersey Railway entrance to the left of the Lyceum Club and Library building, built in 1803 as a gentlemen's club.

Looking up Ranelagh Street, *c.* 1904. The large railway station that was Liverpool Central can be seen on the right and the old Adelphi hotel can be seen at the top of this busy thoroughfare.

The Infirmary for Children, Olive Mount, seen here on a postcard from the early 1900s. The infirmary was built and maintained by the Liverpool Shipping and Cotton Merchants, who were always to the fore in providing for the city's well-being.

The Palm House, Sefton Park, is one of Liverpool's most distinguished landmarks. Thankfully it has received a new lease of life in recent years. This is how it looked in 1900; the postcard was sent as a Christmas card in 1901.

Another view, showing the Palm House dominating Sefton Park.

Henry Yates Thompson paid for the Palm House and gave it as a gift to the people of Liverpool. Many of the statues here have a literary connection. In this view 'Highland Mary' is surrounded by lilies, one of many delights that were to be found inside this lovely Palm House.

25

Liverpool received the news of the death of Queen Victoria in 1901 with great sorrow. Immediately the call went up for a suitable memorial to the late sovereign. The foundation stone for this memorial was laid on 11 October 1902 by Field Marshal Earl Roberts and the architects soon had the contractors working hard on this massive monument paid for by the citizens of Liverpool. This was the scene on 17 September 1906 when the bronze statue of Queen Victoria, sculpted by Charles John Allen, was unveiled by HRH Princess Louise, Duchess of Argyll. To make sure this monument stood out above the tributes of lesser cities, a whole series of allegorical figures were added around and above the Queen. Crowning the dome is a winged figure of Fame and on each cluster of columns stand Justice, Wisdom, Charity and Peace, the Queen's virtues, and round the outer perimeter Agriculture, Industry, Education and Commerce, the glories of her reign.

In 1900 Liverpool began to reclaim what had been St George's Dock. The filling-in of this dock created a wonderful waterfront area on which to build. The intriguing fact is that only one building was started on this new open space and that was the new offices of the Mersey Docks & Harbour Board, seen above. Designed by Arnold Thornley, and taking three years to complete, its construction was watched with interest for there were fears of subsidence. I have been told that the high church dome in the centre was actually designed and started for the Anglican cathedral, but when Thornley lost the contract to design the cathedral he placed the dome here rather than waste the work already done!

The Royal Liver Insurance Company was founded in 1850. The business developed quickly and at the company's Annual Meeting in 1907 it was decided to build a head office to put all other insurance companies to shame. The site chosen was the Liverpool waterfront, and on 11 May 1908 Lord Stanley of Alderley laid the foundation stone for the building that he said would catch the eye of everyone entering the Port of Liverpool. Just to be certain of its foundations, concrete piers were sunk right down to the bed of the old dock, 40 ft below the road surface. It took only three years to build, including the magnificent clock towers surmounted by domes on which the famous 'Liver' birds stand. Aubrey Thomas was the designer of this remarkable building.

A view of the Pier Head and the area on which the Liver Building was built eight years later. The Liverpool Parish Church of Our Lady and St Nicholas stands out in this picture from 1900.

A 1908 photograph of Liverpool's other group of great buildings. Looking up William Brown Street we see, left to right, the College of Technology, the William Brown Library and the Picton Reading Rooms with the Walker Art Gallery away at the top of the street.

28

Bold Street, from an Edwardian postcard, printed in Germany. The Lyceum Club is on the left and St Luke's Church can be seen at the top of the street. At the time Bold Street was *the* street for fashionable shopping.

The new Cotton Exchange, opened by the Prince of Wales on 30 November 1906. This was one of the many great buildings that were destroyed during the blitz of the Second World War.

When Bishop Chavasse was ordained Bishop of Liverpool in 1900 he decided that this 'second city of the Empire' needed a cathedral 'worthy of the people'. On the left we see the pro-cathedral which stood just off Church Street. Below is a rare postcard showing the cathedral as it was to have been, according to the very first plans drawn up by the young Giles Gilbert Scott. He changed the plans just before construction started.

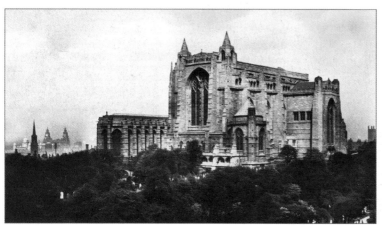

Left: the cathedral under construction.

Above: King Edward VII taps the foundation stone of Liverpool's Anglican cathedral, June 1904. It is said that after the ceremony was over the workers raised the stone again and added a scroll to the treasures already there.

It told of the thousands of people, starving and living in poverty within a mile of this new and costly edifice. True or not I do not know, but it makes a great story.

It is a strange fact that there are not many people living in Liverpool today who have not seen the cathedral at some stage of its construction. It was officially dedicated on 25 October 1978, having taken 74 years in the building. This picture dates from 1932.

31

Shipping from the Pier Head became busier and busier. Here we see a Birkenhead Ferry waiting to load from the old wooden George's Landing Stage.

The view from the top of Liverpool Parish Church, Our Lady and St Nicholas, looking down on the landing stage at the end of the Edwardian period.

The First World War

Many towns and cities in Britain did not feel the impact of the outbreak of the war in 1914 as much as Liverpool. Apart from the raising of the 'Pals' regiments, they were not greatly involved in the early clashes. Liverpool was different: over 25 per cent of its male population were either at sea or involved with the ships that came in and out of the port. Cruise liners were turned into troop carriers, convoys gathered in the Mersey to face submarines in the North Sea, and even the smallest coastal vessel was fitted with guns. Above we see the liner that was one of the greatest losses in the First World War, the *Lusitania*, loading passengers for a cruise just months before war was declared.

Liverpool waterfront at the start of the First World War. The Liver Building and the Dock Office can be seen clearly, and between them the Cunard Building is under construction. Oddly, the Cunard Building is not a true rectangle. It seems that when the foundations were laid it was found that the area had been encroached by the Liver Building. That is why the Cunard Building is 37 ft wider on the landward side than on its Pier Head side. The symbols at the top of the building at the front represent the countries that were Britain's allies on the day war was declared in 1914. They include Russia and Japan.

The Midland Adelphi hotel as it appeared in 1914. It had just been rebuilt and reopened and was the billet of many high-ranking officers during the First World War. 'The day war broke out' (a familiar Liverpool phrase coined by comedian Rob Wilton) at the Adelphi, bed & breakfast would have cost you 14s 6d, a set lunch 4s 6d and dinner 7s 6d: a lot of money in those days when the average weekly wage was about 27s 6d.

Liverpool waterfront and the landing stage, photographed from the newly completed Liver Building. Looking across the river you can see Birkenhead Docks and the Great Float. These docks played a very important role in the First World War. As you can see in this picture the Engineers Memorial has yet to be put in place.

'Holidays at Home' were the order of the day during the war. Here we see a postcard sent in 1916 of the Old Ham and Egg Parade in New Brighton, the scene of many a happy holiday.

Liverpool was still involved with fishing at the time of the First World War and here we see two fishermen mending their nets at the Canning Dock under the gaze of Liverpool's Pier Head trio.

During the First World War Mersey Ferry boats actually went to war. Two of the Wallasey boats (all of which were named after flowers), the *Daffodil* and the *Iris* were chosen to accompany the Royal Navy at their landing at Zeebrugge. Their action was so heroic in blocking the channel that let the German submarines out to sea, that on return they received permission to prefix their ships' names with *Royal*. For many years after we had a *Royal Daffodil* and *Royal Iris* on the River Mersey. In July 1999 it was announced that the *Overchurch* would be renamed *Royal Daffodil (III)* after its recent refit, so the First World War connection is back on the river.

Some of the regiments raised during the First World War were called 'Pals' because the idea was that they went to war with their friends around them. Here we see the Liverpool 'Pals' Barracks at Prescot on a postcard from 1915.

Liverpool Cenotaph was unveiled by Lord Stanley, 17th Earl of Derby on 11 November 1930. The architect was Lionel Bailey Budden and the sculptor George H.T. Smith. It is made of Stancliffe stone and the figures are in bronze. The far side is said to depict the men who went to war and the side seen here shows those left behind to mourn.

Liverpool never stopped sending ships and men to fight for freedom. The losses to the Merchant Navy Fleet were enormous, and almost every Merseyside family had somebody lost at sea. Below we see what is now known as the Engineers Memorial, which stands at the Pier Head. The idea for this memorial was first voiced in 1912 after the sinking of the *Titanic*. The bravery of the Liverpool engineers who stayed at their posts to give the passengers extra minutes to get into the lifeboats struck the imagination of the public, and a fund was started for a 'Titantic Engineers Memorial'. With the outbreak of the First World War and the subsequent loss of many more ships it was decided to make it into a general memorial, as the words inscribed on it say 'In Honour Of All Heroes Of The Marine Engine Room'. It was erected to those brave men in 1916.

Between the Wars

The scene at the George's Pier Head on 2 March 1921. It was named George's Pier Head as
it had been called George's Dock, though whether it was named after a King George or
St George is unclear. The corporation are re-laying tram lines and the area is getting
one of its many facelifts.

Lord Street, Liverpool, around 1920. The tram nearest the camera was painted white and was a 'first class' tram with extra luxurious seating and limited stops.

Derby Square and the Queen Victoria Monument pictured in the 1930s. Trams number 26 and 27, the circular routes, are seen here discharging their passengers. Many tram routes terminated here, and conveniently the lines ran around the monument so that trams could head back out of town without any cumbersome manoeuvres. The trams to Anfield and Goodison Park on match days started from the Victoria Monument.

The 1930s were a time of great change in Liverpool. Many big projects were started in the city centre at this time and here we have two scenes that were to change dramatically in the next few years. This is St John's Gardens and William Brown Street from the Old Haymarket in 1931, just before work was started on the Mersey Tunnel.

A familiar scene from the early 1930s: queues of lorries waiting to cross the river on one of the vehicular ferries, more commonly known as 'luggage ferries'. The tunnel did not open until 1934. The alternative to waiting for the ferry was a 12-mile trip to Widnes to cross the river on the transporter bridge, and then travel 20 miles back to the Wirral to discharge your load. Even more horrendous was the trip to Warrington and the first road bridge crossing of the Mersey. As this was a round trip of over 40 miles, it made the wait at the Pier Head worthwhile.

Two views of the
construction of the Mersey
Tunnel entrance from about
1931. The top view shows
the same area as the top
picture on the previous
page, the Old Haymarket.
The picture below shows
work a little further on and
was taken from the top
of St George's Hall. The
construction of the tunnel
employed 1,700 men who
shifted 1,200,000 tons of
rock and gravel. Much of it
went to Otterspool to make
the promenade there. The
entrances were designed
by Herbert Rouse, who
had studied architecture at
Liverpool.

The official opening of the Queensway Tunnel under the River Mersey took place on 18 July 1934. King George V and Queen Mary declared the tunnel open from the Birkenhead end, and then drove the 2.13 miles through it to take part in an impressive ceremony at the Liverpool end. Above we see the scene at Liverpool just after the arrival of the royal party. Personal photographs taken that day are rare, but below we have two of them. On the left we see the view from the crowd looking towards the platform on which the royal party are seated, and on the right we see the royal couple leaving for their next engagement, which was the opening of the East Lancashire Road.

ENTRANCE TO MERSEY TUNNEL, LIVERPOOL.

MERSEY TUNNEL, (UNDER RIVER MERSEY.)   G.3135.

When the Mersey Tunnel opened there were many postcards and booklets produced to mark this great event. Here we see one of those cards with both a view of the Liverpool entrance and a photograph of the inside of the tunnel. The tunnel has two branches. On the Liverpool side both are still used, but only one way. On the Birkenhead side the Rendel Street Dock Branch has not been used since the 1970s, apart from for a performance by the Liverpool Philharmonic Orchestra in its mouth for the 60th anniversary of the opening of the tunnel in 1994.

When the tunnel was being constructed there was a plan for a tram-line to run underneath the roadway. What you see as you go through the tunnel is just the top half and there is a mirror half below. When it opened the tolls varied according to engine size, with cars under 8hp being charged 1s, while cars over 12hp were charged 2s. At one time there must have been an extra charge relating to the number of passengers carried in cars, as I remember an uncle saying to me, 'Bob down while we go past the toll booth, that will save sixpence.'

Above: All the construction work for the Mersey Tunnel took place below St John's Gardens, yet the adjacent area around Lime Street remained unaffected. Here we see Lime Street around 1928.

The Duke and Duchess of York are seen unveiling the statues of the King and Queen which completed the area at the entrance of the Mersey Tunnel on 6 July 1939, five years after the official opening.

45

The service in Liverpool Cathedral on Easter Sunday morning, 1932. The cathedral was by now was almost half completed, and the main altar and body of the church was in full use. Outside the building work was going ahead well; the tower started to climb in 1930 and was completed by 1939. The work came to a halt for the duration of the Second World War, and the church would remain in this unbalanced state until the 1950s.

Early in the 1930s Liverpool
Corporation sold the site
of the workhouse, and its
grounds, to form the site
of the new Roman Catholic
Cathedral. Edwin Lutyens
was engaged as architect,
and the plan was for a
cathedral to rival St Peter's
in Rome. Here we see an
architect's drawing of how
the cathedral was to look if it
had been completed. Money
was raised and work went
ahead on the crypt of this
wonderful building. Below
we see an aerial view of the
site at Easter 1934 when the
crypt was started. The war
interrupted the work and, as
we know, the original plan
was never completed.

The Children's Garden in Sefton Park, including the Peter Pan statue, on a postcard from 1935. Sefton Park is one of the largest parks in Europe and was started in 1854 when the corporation bought the land from the Earl of Sefton for £264,000. Another £147,000 was spent on laying it out, and the park has provided almost a century and a half of pleasure for the citizens of Liverpool. The Peter Pan statue, which is cast in bronze, was unveiled on 16 June 1928. The work of George Frampton, it is a copy of his earlier one that stands in Kensington Gardens, London.

The iron bridge is another feature of Sefton Park, shown here on a postcard from 1938.

Three views of Liverpool's parks. The city has over one hundred parks. Although the corporation was slow to realise the benefits of providing these green open areas for recreation and pleasure, they made up for it once they had started. This is the Mansion in Calderstones Park, one of the last of the parks to be laid out. The 94 acres include the famous Druids Stone Circle or Calder Stones.

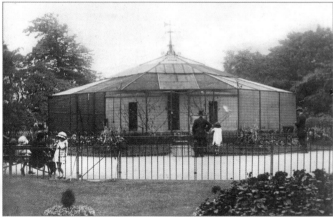

The Aviary in Newsham Park, West Derby. The 131-acre park included the Seamen's Orphanage which did so much good work for the widows and orphans of Liverpool seamen.

Princes Park, at 44 acres one of the city's smaller parks.

Looking up Dale Street away from the town hall, *c.* 1930. Dominating the right-hand side is the Royal Insurance building with its distinctive cupola towers. The building was completed in 1903 after six years of construction to a design by James Francis Doyle. The Prudential Assurance building is beyond, and dominating the far end of the street with its clock tower is the Municipal Buildings, built in 1866 and irreverently nicknamed the 'Bedpost Palace.' I have heard it referred to as the Civic Hall and the Town Hall Extension – some people even think it is the Town Hall. This building was designed by John Weightman, the corporation surveyor, and is a wonderful mixture of styles and tastes.

The Pier Head, 1930. What a high tide, as our photographer takes a picture of the 'Three Graces' which greet visitors to the port. On the Cunard Building in the middle of the uppermost storey are carved the arms of Britain's allies in the First World War. These are not named but include the arms of France, Russia, Japan, Belgium, Serbia and Montenegro.

An atmospheric picture of a tram passing beneath the overhead railway, next to the Pier Head station, en route to the terminus at the waterfront.

Above: One of the highlights of the year is the Grand National. Here we see a packed line of trams in Warbreck Moor, Aintree, on a race day in 1925.

Lord Derby leads his horse Hyperion into the winners' enclosure at Royal Ascot in 1933. The 17th Earl was a popular figure in racing circles and liked by the people of Merseyside. Any horse carrying his colours was bound to attract a few bets from the locals and his wins were popular.

The May Day Parade (of horses and firms) was very popular between the wars. Here we see the parade passing Bunney's Corner, *c.* 1933.

Liverpool Airport opened on 1 July 1932 with a great Air Pageant heralding a new age of transport on Merseyside. This is Liverpool's first air freight transport plane, a de Havilland Dragon, pictured in 1934. It is being loaded with sausages from the Richmond Sausage Company, Litherland, for delivery to the south of England.

Liverpool Stadium just days before it opened in October 1932. The stadium could seat 4,000 people and was the scene of many notable events besides the boxing matches for which it was built. Jerry Lee Lewis played a rock concert there and Hogan 'Kid' Bassey, Dick Tiger and Billy Ellaway were among the boxers who appeared in fights at this venue. The Liverpool Philharmonic used it to give concerts for schoolchildren.

The Duchess of York presents the FA Cup to Everton's captain Dixie Dean after his team beat Manchester City 3–0 at Wembley in 1933.

St George's Hall, *c.* 1935. This impressive building was constructed not only as a public concert hall but also as law courts. Many famous trials took place here including the Maybrick case. Florence Maybrick, who lived in a house overlooking Liverpool cricket ground in Grassendale, was found guilty of murdering her husband James (whom many suspect could have been Jack the Ripper) and had her death sentence commuted at the very last moment because she was an American. She still spent fifteen years in Walton Prison and only came back to Liverpool once in the 1920s to watch the Grand National.

The Exchange Flags, with the Liverpool Exchange behind, as they appeared in the years between the wars. The large round monument in the centre of the Flags is the Nelson Memorial, Liverpool's first public sculpture, erected in 1813. The chained figures represent prisoners taken after Nelson's four great victories at Cape St Vincent, the Nile, Copenhagen and Trafalgar.

The top of London Road, 1922. The statue of George III had by this time been moved from its original position to a specially laid-out park opened here in 1910.

The Library and Museum on William Brown Street, and St John's Gardens. The gardens are named after St John's Church which stood here from 1783 to 1887. The churchyard was converted into a public garden in 1904, and contains more statues in its 3.25 acres than anywhere else in Europe, which led to it being nicknamed the Stoneyard.

Above: Lord Street, *c.* 1930. Every building on the left of this picture was destroyed during the blitz of the Second World War.

The ornate Cotton Exchange, another victim of Hitler's rebuilding programme for Liverpool.

An aerial view of Liverpool's waterfront and some of the docks just before the outbreak of the Second World War. Custom House can be seen dominating the end of Paradise Street. Princes Dock has two Irish boats in it, and the Albert Dock looks busy and working. At the top of the picture are the unloading sheds and warehouses on the Kings Dock, with Queens Branch Dock beyond.

Above: Liverpool Town Hall, late 1920s. The building we see here is the same today and is the fourth Town Hall to be built on this spot. The postcard's original caption says Town Hall and Martin's Bank, but we now know it as Barclays Bank. It was to this bank that the gold reserves were brought and stored in vaults in the basement after the collapse of France in 1940. A plaque on the front of the building records this event when 280 tons of gold in 4,719 boxes were kept here for a month before being shipped to Canada, where they remained until after the war.

Looking down Church Street towards the Pier Head in the 1930s.

Workers waiting for their train at Nelsons Dock Station on the Liverpool Overhead Railway. It is one of Liverpool's great regrets that not more was done to save the Overhead Railway. It was still carrying 10,000,000 passengers a year in the 1950s but needed £2 million spent on it to bring it up to safety standards. As the private company that owned it was not able to find that money, the railway closed and within 12 months the whole thing had vanished.

Once a year the overhead railway would be extended and run into Sefton Arms station at Aintree for the Grand National meeting. This service carried thousands of people to and from the racecourse, taking pressure off the trams and buses. Here we see one of the old-type overhead railway cars standing at Aintree station on 24 March 1956. *(Photo: A.C. Gilbert)*

As the end of the 1930s approached, Liverpool made plans to get rid of its trams. The service was run using old and worn out vehicles which were kept operating until buses could be ordered. In the event, war put paid to these modernisation plans and the trams were cannibalised even more in an attempt to keep them going. Here we see an old-style round-ended tram with one of the new 'Baby Grands' in August 1937.

A stark picture of tram number 127 waiting to set out on the No. 4 route down Penny Lane to Wavertree, c. 1938.

Ranelagh Street, just before the outbreak of the Second World War. The new look Lewis's is at the top of the street on the right. This building was the brainchild of Louis Cohen, who died in 1922 before it was completed in 1924. He had been Lord Mayor of Liverpool in 1899 and always had grand plans for the company he started in 1910.

Looking down from St George's Hall to the tunnel entrance, summer 1939. This postcard was printed in 1940 and has on it a stirring message from the Prime Minister: 'Let us all strive without failing in faith or in duty.'

A Life on the
Ocean Wave

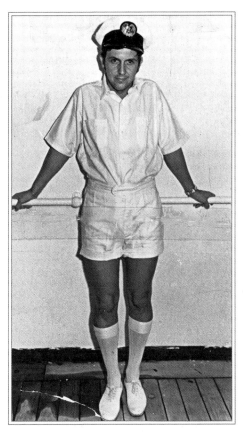

Liverpool is married to the Mersey, that's a fact. Sir Archibald Salvidge threw a large wedding ring into the Mersey in 1928 to make it official. In days gone by a large proportion of the men of Liverpool were part of that marriage. They staffed the ocean liners, they were the sailors on Royal Navy ships, they were the baggage handlers and dockers loading and unloading the 'Queens of the Ocean'. Merseyside men did not need passports to take on their journeys round the world, but they did need a Discharge Book. Here is a photo from my sea-faring days.

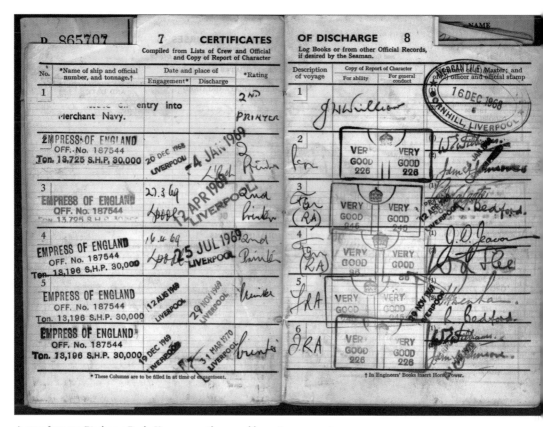

A page from my Discharge Book. You can see the resemblance to a passport.

The Shaw Saville ship the *Ocean Monarch* at the oiling berth at Rock Ferry after its refit in Birkenhead in 1970–71. This ship started life as the *Empress of England*, one of Canadian Pacific's *Great White Empresses* that graced the River Mersey for so many years. Sold to Shaw Saville in 1968, she had spent twelve months cruising from Australia to Japan before coming back for a refit, and replacing the male waiters with waitresses before steaming off for another season of cruising. I was the ship's printer and my wife was one of those waitresses.

<table>
<tr><td colspan="4" align="center">SATURDAY SAILINGS</td></tr>
<tr><td colspan="4" align="center">LIVERPOOL TO LONDON</td></tr>
</table>

SATURDAY SAILINGS

LIVERPOOL TO LONDON

LIVERPOOL (Bramley Moore Dock)		Depart Saturday	as above
PLYMOUTH ... Arrive Monday a.m.		Depart Monday	p.m.
SOUTHAMPTON ... Arrive Tuesday a.m.		Depart Tuesday	p.m.
LONDON ... Arrive Wednesday p.m. (tide)			

LONDON TO LIVERPOOL

LONDON (The Jetty, London Docks)		Depart Saturday	as above
PLYMOUTH ... Arrive Monday a.m.		Depart Monday	p.m.
LIVERPOOL ... Arrive Wednesday a.m.			

WEDNESDAY SAILINGS

LIVERPOOL TO LONDON.

LIVERPOOL (Bramley Moore Dock)		Depart Wednesday	as above
FALMOUTH ... Arrive Friday a.m.		Depart Friday	p.m.
PLYMOUTH ... Arrive Saturday a.m.		Depart Saturday	p.m.
LONDON ... Arrive Sunday p.m. (tide)			

LONDON TO LIVERPOOL

LONDON (The Jetty, London Docks)		Depart Wednesday	as above
SOUTHAMPTON ... Arrive Friday a.m.		Depart Friday	p.m.
FALMOUTH ... Arrive Saturday a.m.		Depart Saturday	p.m.
LIVERPOOL ... Arrive Sunday p.m.			

	Intermediate Seasons 13th April to 28th May and 10th September to 8th October (All dates inclusive).		High Season 1st June to 7th September (Inclusive).	
LIVERPOOL/LONDON	£3 10 0	£5 5 0	£4 5 0	£6 10 0
LIVERPOOL/FALMOUTH... ...	£2 5 0	£3 5 0	£2 10 0	£4 0 0
LIVERPOOL/PLYMOUTH... ...	£2 10 0	£3 10 0	£2 15 0	£4 5 0
LIVERPOOL/SOUTHAMPTON ...	£3 0 0	£4 10 0	£3 10 0	£5 10 0
PLYMOUTH/SOUTHAMPTON ...	£1 5 0	£2 10 0	£1 10 0	£3 0 0
PLYMOUTH/LONDON	£2 10 0	£3 15 0	£2 15 0	£4 10 0
SOUTHAMPTON/LONDON ...	£1 5 0	£2 10 0	£1 10 0	£3 0 0
LONDON/FALMOUTH	£2 15 0	£4 0 0	£3 0 0	£4 10 0
FALMOUTH/LIVERPOOL... ...	£2 5 0	£3 5 0	£2 10 0	£4 0 0
SOUTHAMPTON/FALMOUTH ...	£1 10 0	—	£1 15 0	

The years between the wars saw a rise in coastal cruising. Companies did not visit foreign ports but used a luxury liner to transport you round the coast of Britain. There were regular services from Liverpool to Glasgow as well as the service shown in the brochure above which left every Wednesday and Saturday for Southampton and London. Maybe it was a long way round – 644 miles by sea Liverpool to London – but you had two days of relaxation, good food and entertainment before arriving refreshed at your destination.

Here we see some of the entertainment provided on these coastal cruises. Passengers are taking part in a 'Washing the Baby' competition aboard the SS *Lancastria* in May 1934.

THE SPORTS & SOCIAL CLUB OF THE

S.S. SOUTHERN CROSS

PRESENT A

GRAND OUTDOOR
BOXING EXHIBITION

By kind permission of
Captain W. M. Wheatley

ON THE SUNDECK

SUNDAY 6th JUNE 1971   AT 9.00 p.m.

The crew were expected not only to serve but to entertain as well. One of the highlights of a cruise would be a crew boxing match. With the usual mixture of Liverpool deckhands and Irish and Scottish waiters, every ship could lay on a tough bout or two. Above left we see a crew boxing match on the *Lancastria* in 1934, while on the right is the cover of a programme for a boxing match aboard the SS *Southern Cross* in June 1971 while crossing the Indian Ocean.

Sport was important to crew members; it kept morale up and many times a football match would keep them out of trouble in a foreign port. So many liners sailed into Montreal, Canada, during the summer months that the shipping companies sponsored a Montreal Cup to be played for by the football teams from the liners. This motley crew is the team and reserves from the *Empress of England* after they had won the Montreal Cup and other silverware, displayed here in 1968.

The liners that left Liverpool in the inter-war years and during the 1950s and '60s provided a service that was second-to-none. Not only did these ships carry hairdressers, keep-fit instructors, nurses and nannies, but printers as well. This is some of the handywork of those printers, who provided 'hot off the press' news and information for passengers as well as the daily menus and other printed matter to keep the ship running smoothly. I once sailed with a 'Ship's Gardener' whose sole job it was to raise flowers and plants in a large plastic greenhouse tucked away behind the funnels. He produced fresh flowers for the captain's table and bouquets of daffodils for ladies' birthdays.

Liverpool crews were proud of their ships and the service they provided. In port a liner always looked slightly dusty and not at her best, but once those ropes were let go, and the ship was out at sea it was soon sparkling again. Above we see the tourist smoking room on the *Empress of England* as it was in 1965. Below is the St Laurent Restaurant on the same ship.

Above: the cocktail bar on the *Empress of Britain* in 1960. Gin and whisky were 1s a tot, and 20 cigarettes cost 2s. There were so many liners with Liverpool crews that the *Daily Post and Echo* had shipping columns telling where each of the Liverpool boats was. In the *Daily Post* you could follow each ship as it sailed the world, noting the day and date of each port of call. The *Echo* provided daily lists of all arrivals and departures from the port. 'I knew you were coming home, I saw it in the *Echo*' were words used to greet many seamen as they slipped into their local after a long sea voyage. Below is the *Empress of Scotland* coming alongside the landing stages. *c.* 1950.

MERSEYSIDE SHIPPING

KEY—L (left/leaves), A (arrived), F (for), P (passed), S (sailed), D (due), C (called), B (berthed)

Blue Funnel Line
ACHILLES C Aden May 7.
AJAX A Singapore May 7.
ANCHISES L Swansea May 9.
ANTENOR A Dublin May 8.
AUTOMEDON D Penang May 8.
CLYTONEUS C Penang May 7.
IDOMENEUS A Penang May 8.
PYRRHUS L Singapore May 7.
RAUNDORSHIRE A Singapore May 8
RHESUS A Penang May 8.
SARPEDON L Hong Kong May 7.
TEUCER A Singapore May 7.

Hall Line
CITY OF LEEDS L Mangalore May 9.
C. BEDFORD L Busy May 9.
C. BATH L Karachi May 6
C. OTTAWA L Gibraltar May 10
O. GUILDFORD A Bombay May 8.
C. JOHANNESBURG L Fremantle May 8.
C. STAFFORD L Koweit May 8.
C. WINNIPEG L Calcutta May 8.
C. CARLISLE L Port Sudan May 9.
C SINGAPORE L Hull May 10.

H. E. Moss & Co. Tankers
LUMEN D Persian Gulf May 25.
LUCERNA D Banias May 21.
LUSTROUS A Falmouth May 10.
LUCELLU D Dakar May 14.

Larrinaga Steamship Co.
RAMON DE LARRINAGA L Dub. May 8.

A packed Gladstone Dock in the early 1950s. One of the highlights of a visit to Liverpool was to see the liners. While the Overhead Railway was running it was one of the selling points that a return journey on the overhead gave a great view of the ships in the docks.

The *Empress of Scotland* tied up in Liverpool, April 1950. In the 1940s and '50s there were as many a twenty large liners sailing regularly from Liverpool. The ships themselves had fascinating stories to tell, and the atmosphere aboard each one was different. The *Empress of Scotland* had actually started life in December 1929 as the *Empress of Japan* and had spent many years out in the Pacific before becoming a troop carrier during the Second World War. Renamed the *Empress of Scotland* she carried on as a troop ship until 1948. She was then refitted and commenced the Liverpool to North America service. In December 1951 she brought the Queen and Duke of Edinburgh back from their visit to Canada. She was laid up in December 1957 and sold on as the *Hanseatic*.

A busy landing stage on a Sunday morning in 1956. The *St Tudno* is nearest the camera with passengers going aboard for their day excursion to far-flung Llandudno. Note the crew gangway nearest the camera and the cook having a quick 'smoko' before going back into the galley. Behind is the Cunard liner *Carinthia* which was scheduled to leave the following day for New York.

Services to *all* parts of the world sailed from the Mersey. Here we see a liner leaving for the Amazon and Rio de Janeiro in 1933.

All Merchant Navy personnel had uniforms and as well as the Naval Outfitters, Lewis's sold the required clothing, from captains' uniforms to galley-boys' checks.

The Isle of Man Steamship Company has long provided a service from Liverpool to Douglas, Isle of Man. Above we see the SS *Tynwald* just after the Second World War when holidays on the island were very popular. On the right is the cover menu of the last sailing of the *Manxman* and below is a postcard of the SS *Mona's Queen* from the 1950s.

Souvenir Luncheon Menu

to mark

The Last Passenger Sailing

of the

S.S. MANXMAN

MANXMAN STEAMER SOCIETY

Sailing
Liverpool to Douglas to Liverpool
on the
4th September, 1982

The service to Belfast and Dublin has always been an important one for Liverpool. This is one of the Belfast boats, the *Logie*, loading at the landing stage before returning to Belfast in 1911.

These are two of the Mersey Ferries, the *Marlowe* above and the *Egremont* to the right. At one time the ferries were run by two different corporations. Birkenhead Corporation ran the service from Birkenhead to Liverpool, while Wallasey Corporation ran their service from Seacombe and New Brighton. I always thought it was strange that Liverpool Corporation took no part in the Ferry Services.

The Birkenhead ferry approaches the floating landing stage at Birkenhead with the Liver buildings across the river behind it.

The ferry waits at the landing stage. These ferry boats not only provided a journey across the river but laid on trips to Manchester via the Ship Canal and Pop and Jazz Cruises at weekends. Top acts of the time such as the Beatles, Acker Bilk and Kenny Ball and his Jazzmen were among those who performed on these popular cruises.

Liverpool
and the Blitz

The first air raid on Liverpool was on the night of 17/18 August 1940.
One of the city's first casualties was the LMS Goods Station, Caryl
Street, seen here being cleared up the following morning.

Above: It was not only Liverpool city centre that received the attention of the German Luftwaffe. Because the docks stretched to the north and south of the city, Bootle and Garston received their share of bombings. This is a street in Bootle showing the damage that one high explosive bomb could do.

This is what was left of the Engineering Department of Liverpool University after the May Blitz.

Volunteer firemen fight a blaze on
St George's Crescent, Liverpool,
May 1941.

Digging out victims was a task
that had to be done quickly and
with great care. Here we see an
ARP team checking recently
bombed houses.

Cook Street arcade in the very heart
of Liverpool stands burnt out and
still smouldering.

The Corn Exchange may have disappeared into a pile of rubble but the dealers and workers gather outside what little remained of their once-beautiful workplace, to carry on with vital work.

The Railway Goods Depot at Waterloo burning fiercely, Christmas 1940. The remains of the building stand out against the flames that illuminate the sky over Liverpool.

William Brown Museum after the Blitz.

The amount of damage inflicted on Liverpool city centre and outlying areas is hard to imagine since the devastation was spread far and wide. Whole streets disappeared and magnificent buildings, homes, churches, schools – nothing was sacred – were reduced to masses of rubble. The view above looks over the top of the Queen Victoria Memorial and up Church Street. The photograph below, taken from an RAF plane, shows the Pier Head area and the vast areas of damage behind it, June 1941.

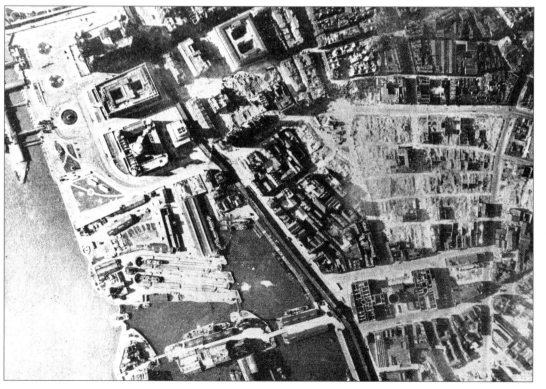

A convoy of ships gathers in grey wartime colours ready to face the German U-boats in the North Atlantic.

Above: It was not only the men who were involved in war work on the docks. Here women of the Mersey Docks & Harbour Board canteen are preparing to serve breakfast after another hard night.

Left: The start of the American 'invasion' and a Jeep being unloaded at Liverpool Docks ready to be taken to Burton Wood Air Base.

This picture shows the scene of utter and complete devastation following the disaster involving the Brocklebank ship the *Malakand*. On 2 May 1941 in Huskisson No. 2 Dock, the *Malakand* was loaded with 1,000 tons of shells and bombs for the Middle East. She caught fire and after four hours of battling, the firemen had to retreat. Minutes after they left the ship blew up taking with it the warehouses on either side. An area of almost one square mile was completely flattened. Miraculously nobody was killed.

Number 2 Shed on the Canada Dock after a direct hit by enemy bombs.

The docks at Liverpool worked day and night bringing in supplies and materials for the war effort. It did not seem possible that any more could be handled yet, when the Americans came, all their supplies were received through Liverpool too. Above we see steam locos after unloading at Birkenhead Docks. Below, the giant crane 'Mammoth' lifts a 200-ton tugboat from the deck of an American cargo boat to give it its first taste of the River Mersey. Most of these goods imported from America were on what was called Lease Lend to be paid for after the war. On the right we see the battle by firefighters to keep the warehouses intact.

A famous photograph of the nerve centre from which the Naval Operations for the whole of the North Atlantic were conducted. The Western Approaches Command opened in February 1941 in the bowels of Derby House – officially known as 'The Citadel'. It is now a major tourist attraction called 'Western Approaches'.

The story of war-time hero Captain F.J. 'Johnny' Walker, a popular naval officer responsible for the protection of the convoys out of Liverpool, is one worth looking up and reading about. His devotion to duty, courage and tenacity is legendary. The fact that there is now a statue in his honour, looking out over his beloved River Mersey is testament to how much he was revered by all who served with him. Behind this statue is the Merchant Navy War Memorial to the Missing of the Naval Auxiliary Personnel of the Second World War.

This statue was commissioned by Captain Walker's Old Boys Association, sculpted by Tom Murphy and unveiled by H.R.H. The Duke of Edinburgh KG, KT on 16th October 1998

Austerity and Aftermath

The scene in Lime Street on VE Day, 8 May 1945. Ironically in the middle of the picture stands the Cenotaph from the First World War, 'the war that was to end all wars'. Though Victory in Europe was expected for some days before, there was still much confusion when the day arrived. The government had not decided to make the official announcement until late on 7 May, so many people turned up for work as usual only to be told of the enforced holiday and sent home. Many did not go and stayed in the city centre to hear the news 'live' later at lunchtime. Public houses and hotels opened early to accommodate the crowds, and as the good news spread the limited beer and spirits supply soon ran out. Long before the end of the day, many a dusty bottle was dragged out of the back of the pub shelves. 'What yer got to drink? Go on, I'll have one of those.' Crowds thronged the streets to express their relief that the war was finally over.

After the war a committee was formed to oversee the planning and rebuilding of Liverpool city centre. Many plans were put forward and the debates raged on as to how the city would go forward. Here we see a model of one of the plans put forward with St George's Hall at the bottom centre and the Mersey Tunnel entrance in the middle of model.

Many of the photographs taken in the
1950s show levelled-out bomb sites behind
whatever was being photographed. This
picture was taken to record tram number
222 on the 19A route service to South
Dene from Church Street. The picture
picks up two of the cleared areas almost
by accident. The Major cinema behind the
tram is showing Spencer Tracy in
Bad Day at Black Rock.

One of the new buses stands in Canning
Place ready to head out all the way to
Leeds on the resumed bus service, early
1950s.

A picture of the war-damaged Custom
House as it stood for many years after the
war as a reminder of the Blitz.

The Anfield dressing room at the start of the 1946/7 season, showing players changing for a match. Note the numbered coat pegs and the famous massage table in the middle of the room.

An action shot from the 1946/7 season. Stubbins scores for Liverpool in a cup tie against Birmingham City at Anfield.

Liverpool players always lunched at Birkdale before a home match. Here we see Jack Balmer (the Liverpool captain) signing the menu as team mates Hughes, Paisley, Jones and Priday enjoy their soup.

A scene from the Everton dressing room as their Manager Theo Kelly chats to Ted Sagar before a match in 1946.

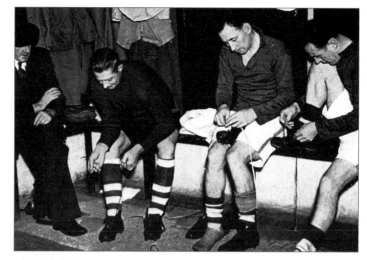

Below: Catterick of Everton challenges Aston Villa goalkeeper Rutherford in a tense situation at Goodison Park, 1947.

Below, right: Saunders, Everton's full back, watches as goalkeeper Ted Sagar saves a shot from Blackpool forward McKnight in the 1946/7 season.

A view of the Pier Head area in 1955. The cleared bombed areas can still be made out even though much rebuilding had already taken place.

Liverpool's Parker Street in 1955. The view has changed since this picture was taken with the building of the St John's Centre.

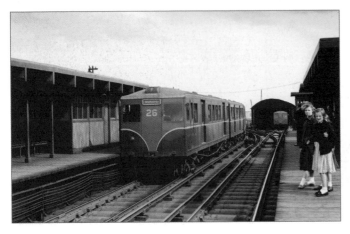

The Liverpool Overhead Railway was very important during the war for moving men from dock to dock and getting people to work, so any damage done to it was quickly put right. After the war it did not seem so important and by 1955 it had assumed a shabby, worn appearance. Here some young ladies wait on Herculaneum Station for the next train for Dingle. (*Photo A.C. Gilbert*)

The one thing that the bomb sites did help with was the parking, as we can see here in 1952.

Central station is approached through long deep tunnels, and here we see the entrance to these tunnels during reconstruction work just after the war. (*Locofotos*)

There had been few holidays during the war but the time between 1946 and 1950 saw the reappearance of motor coaches on their routes to North Wales' beaches.

Modernisation was the byword at the end of the 1940s. To be clean and modern was all the rage. Here we see a waitress attending to the requirements of these happy imbibers at the newly modernised Ring O' Bells Hotel, West Kirby in 1947.

The feeling of renewal and rebuilding after the war sometimes led to places being cleared away just for the sake of being new and modern. Here is a quiet scene of a gentleman enjoying his pint of mild in the Childwall Abbey Hotel in 1946, still left untouched for the time being.

After the war, women felt that as they had stood shoulder-to-shoulder with the men throughout the war, they had won the right to more social freedom for themselves. Here we see a lady joining the men in the snug of the Anchor Hotel, Irby, for a quick game of darts in 1946.

Liverpool Swings

The spirit of the swinging sixties really began on Merseyside in the fifties.
The Festival of Britain had been thoroughly embraced by Liverpool and when the Coronation
came along, everyone was ready for a good street party. This one is at Teulon Street, Walton.

The story of Liverpool music scene in the swinging sixties is well recorded in over a dozen books. The fact that I was there in the middle of it helps me look back on it as a time of discovery. There were hundreds of groups and dozens of places where they could show off their developing talent. We discovered that girls were more interested in you if you were 'in a group', and for every lad who was in a group there were another three who were 'just about to form one'. We discovered that you really could get a whole drum kit under the stairs of a corporation bus . . . if you tried very hard, that picking up a piece of equipment and mumbling 'I'm with the group' sometimes got you in free, that it was a long walk home from Huyton, etc.

This photo fell out of a file lent to me some years ago by Medley and Bird and it is not known who the group are. So like the unknown soldier, this photo represents all the thousands who formed groups in the 1960s, those who never got a recording contract, or made it to *Top of the Pops*, the stories of how they almost made it, or played the same bill as The Beatles or The Searchers . . . 'And this girl told me we were better than them – honest'.

The film *Ferry Across the Mersey* was first shown in 1962, and both the film and the song have been firm favourites on Merseyside ever since. Here we see Gerry Marsden on the landing stage during the making of that film. Other members of the Pacemakers, including his brother Les, are in the background. (*Daily Post*)

A private photo taken off the balcony of the Tower Ballroom, New Brighton, on the night that the Rolling Stones appeared there. The night was sponsored by Rael-Brooke Toplin shirts and there were girls in just shirts dancing at the back of the stage for most of the night. Here we see bouncers trying to clear the crush at the front of the stage just prior to the Stones coming on.

Football legend Dixie Dean leads out the Liverpool and Everton teams for a derby in the 1963/4 season. Ron 'Rowdy' Yates is the Liverpool captain and Tommy Lawrence, the goalkeeper, can be clearly seen behind him. The Everton team are being led out by Tony Kay who only stayed at the club a couple of years before leaving in disgrace. Dixie was a football hero who was admired by both sides of Liverpool. He passed away at his beloved Goodison in March of 1980.

Opposite, bottom: Local radio is listened to more on Merseyside than anywhere else in the country. In the '60s Radio Merseyside was a popular station and gave first airing and interviews to many local groups and personalities including the legendary Beatles. Some of those '60s rockers are still around today and still providing great entertainment though sometimes in a different capacity. One such lad was Billy Butler, one-time member of the Tuxedoes, who got a television break on the panel of *Thank Your Lucky Stars* and later teamed up with his radio producer Wally Scott to come up with the hilarious *Hold Your Plums* radio quiz show. This show had to be heard to be believed and tapes of it can be found with exiled Scousers all over the world. It was Butler's cleverness in phrasing the questions so that everyone except the contestant knew the answer that made those contestants seem thick. 'What was Hitler's first name?' – 'Was it Heil, Billy' is typical of the show. Here we see Wally Scott (left) and Billy Butler (right) with another radio stalwart Billy Mahr in the centre, relaxing in the Moat House in 1994. Billy had just had a book published about a letter his wife had written about his DIY disasters and it had been received very well by the people who listened to his show on Radio Merseyside. Billy and Wally have moved about the airwaves a little, having been on both BBC and commercial radio. They are two very decent lads and deserve their popularity.

'Our Cilla', born Priscilla White in Scotland Road, Liverpool, now known the world over as Cilla Black, television host presenter and still a good singer when she needs to be. She is seen here when she reached 21 and had a swinging, fab groovy party, with all her show-business friends and colleagues. (*Daily Post and Echo*).

The Seventies to the Present Day

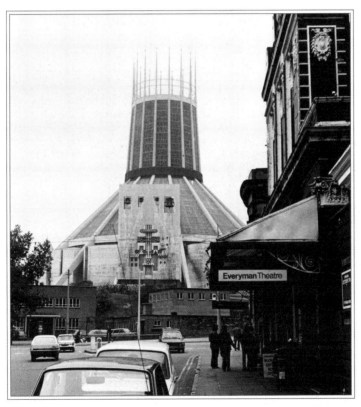

The 1970s signalled an era of stark changes in Liverpool's fortunes. This was the decade when much of the cargo shipping stopped coming into the port, due in part to economic circumstances and containerisation. At the start of the '70s there were few cruise liners left as Cunard had moved to Southampton – it was not long before Canadian Pacific did the same. This was the end of an era. But there were some good things happening in Liverpool. The opening of the Everyman Theatre, the completion of the Roman Catholic Cathedral, and an initiative to reclaim and reinvent the Albert Dock as a living and pleasure area were all in the pipeline. Here we see the Everyman Theatre just after it opened, with the newly completed Metropolitan Cathedral of Christ the King in the background.

Cammell Laird had been busy during the 1960s with contracts from the MOD for nuclear submarines. They were known as Polaris submarines and the yard built four of them. Above we see the last of those, HMS *Revenge*, being launched into the River Mersey in December of 1969. They cost almost £40million each, and kept alive the yard's record for building submarines. The workforce at Cammell Laird at the time was around 12,000. Little did the workers realise how soon the yard would face problems – with government interference and repeated threats of closure, shipbuilding would almost completely disappear from a river that once boasted eight shipyards.

The Green Lane entrance gates to the Cammell Laird Shipyard over in Birkenhead, complete with its figure of Britannia and models of ships that had been built there. The one on the right is the *Mauritania*. Cammell Laird closed down in 1993, but reopened, surviving until 2001.

Above: You can't do a book about Liverpool without a picture of Bill Shankly in it. I have had to omit so many other Merseyside legends, but Bill had to go in. Bill Shankly joined Liverpool as manager in December 1959, and they were made for each other. His quotes are famous and his wit was razor sharp. After his retirement things were not always at their best between him and the club, but there is no doubt that Shankly was the man who made Liverpool the great club it is today. When he died in 1981 Liverpool was robbed of a great character, and the Shankly Gates at Anfield are a fitting tribute to the great man. (*Liverpool Echo*)

Kenny Dalglish, who joined Liverpool from Celtic in August 1977 for the then record fee of £440,000. He was bought to take the place of Kevin Keegan and soon made himself a favourite with the Anfield faithful. He caught the spirit of the late seventies and was a thoughtful player with a high work rate. In 1985 Kenny took over as manager of the club and with 100 Scottish caps behind him he managed to carry on Liverpool's success. The mystery of his departure still has not been truly solved, but this should not distract from his service to the 'Reds' as both player and manager. (*Liverpool Echo*)

The Royal Yacht *Britannia* pictured in the River Mersey on 20 June 1977. Tugs manoeuvre the liner to the landing stage at the start of a royal visit.

The *QEII* arriving in the River Mersey on her first visit to the port, 24 July 1990. She came to celebrate Cunard's 150th anniversary.

Walking down the pier at New Brighton, having just got off the ferry from Liverpool and looking forward to good day out. There was everything you could wish for at New Brighton: a large outdoor swimming pool, bowling greens, paddling, miniature railway, boating lake, and all the fun of the large fairground there. Another scene that vanished in the 1970s was the ferry to New Brighton – its last sailing was on Sunday 26 September 1971.

St George's Hall, late 1970s. St John's Shopping Precinct had been completed and Roe Street had six lanes of traffic. The Playhouse theatre can be seen on the right of the picture.

Steam engines always seem more exciting when they carry a name plate; they seem more important. The name *Liverpool* has been carried by quite a few engines, large and small over the years. Here we see London Midland Scottish engine No. 7334 *Liverpool* at Edge Hill Motive Power depot in 1932. The engine was a saddle tank, and probably stayed local for short trips and shunting duty. *(Locofotos)*

Nothing local about this engine, LMS engine no. 46247 *City of Liverpool* built in 1937. Originally this engine was streamlined and looked as the preserved ER steam engine *Mallard* does today. This picture is from the early 1950s as you can still make out the slope on the front of the boiler that shows the engine was streamlined, yet the tender is not marked 'BR' as they were after the 1960s. *(Locofotos)*

In 1930 there was a large celebration held in Liverpool to mark the centenary of the opening of the Liverpool–Manchester Railway. At that time many of the fastest engines in Britain gathered in Liverpool and the public flocked to see them. Some local engines were named to mark the occasion and here we see one of those, *Liverpool Engineer*, at Edge Hill sheds (8A) in 1932. (*Locofotos*)

Liverpool Central was a busy station. It could hold its head up against Lime Street (for London and south) and Exchange (for Scotland and north). Trains ran to Manchester, and all stations to Warrington, and also expresses to Hull and Parkiston Quay for the boat trains to the Hook of Holland.

Riverside railway station, built especially to service the transatlantic liners and the cruise ships that sailed from Liverpool. The station closed down in the 1960s, and was cleared away in the early '70s. Trains were always awkward to run from here as the line ran over many dock bridges and weight limits were crucial. It then ran from the dock goods station in tunnels under Liverpool for five miles, coming out at Edge Hill.

St John's Beacon was the official title given to the tall tower with a revolving restaurant on top that can be seen above St John's shopping centre and the rest of Liverpool city centre. Finished about the end of 1966, it is now the home of Radio City. I was rather disappointed when I learned that it was built as the chimney for the boilers of the St John's Precinct and the restaurant was just added as an afterthought. I always thought it was like London's Post Office Tower, built for some lofty purpose.

This is the view from the revolving bit at the top of the Beacon just after it opened, *c.* 1969. The picture above looks down on St George's Hall and Lime Street station across the road. The one on the left shows the view towards the Anglican Cathedral. Lewis's can be seen at the bottom left of the picture and the approach to Central station is just behind it.

Three more views from the Tower in about 1969: a wonderful record of Liverpool at the time. You can study them with a magnifying glass and find lots to talk about on every one. At the top, we see the Roman Catholic cathedral that had been dedicated in 1967 and where Pope John Paul II captivated the hearts of the people in May 1982. Below that we see the Queensway tunnel entrance, uncluttered as it was then, and the gardens and William Brown Street behind. The bottom picture looks towards the Pier Head and the famous trio there. You can see the Queen Elizabeth law courts being built with two cranes surrounding the site.

Words are inadequate to describe this picture. It is a memory that will stay with us all, as long as we live. I hope that those who lost loved ones, among the 96 who died as a result of that terrible day at Hillsborough in April 1989, can take some small comfort in the thought that thousands of other people on Merseyside and further afield are grieving along with them, even today. They will get the answers they are looking for and the justice they deserve.

109

Looking down Park Road Toxteth, away from the 'Holy Land' towards town in the 1970s. Moses Street, Isaac Street and Jacob Street are just behind the photographer. The Toxteth pub stands out on the corner and though the district was hard, no one was prepared for the trouble that was to come.

The same street, but this is 1981 – the year of the Toxteth riots. It wasn't only Toxteth that suffered. Bristol and Manchester had riots as well, but the troubles in Liverpool always seem to be discussed more. The strong bonds between the two faiths in Liverpool and the fact that church leaders wanted to go in and talk to the people, who were prepared to listen, stopped the situation becoming worse. (*Liverpool Echo*)

The eighties saw, at last, a tackling of the city's problem district of Liverpool 8. Here we see Upper Parliament Street in the Percy Street area and the large houses up there are much in need of a little 'Tender Loving Care'.

Even in the twenty-first century there are bits of Liverpool that still reflect the hammering it received during the Second World War. This picture was taken in 1969 to show 'The Pub That Stood Alone' and it's still there today near the Liverpool University complex.

My hero in local broadcasting, Bob Azurdia, seen here getting a programme ready for broadcast, *c.* 1985. Bob was the first person to interview me on radio in 1985, and made me feel at ease right from the start. Even though I had never been on radio before Bob gave me a full half hour, chatting and telling of the books I was involved with and plans for the future. I had worked with him at the *Liverpool Weekly News* in the late 1960s, and can only remember him as a hard-working, easy to get on with colleague. His death in 1996 was a shock to everyone. He had been running in a half-marathon for charity – he took part in many. He is sadly missed.

Anybody who is anybody can be found down at the local BBC radio station. I did four years, every Wednesday afternoon, with presenter Linda MacDermott and recorded another piece for broadcast on Sunday nights with Maureen Walsh. I can honestly say I have sat next to Linda Lusardi, P.J. Proby and Ken Dodd. I have had to move up to let Boyzone sit down and chatted to the Revd David Sheppard, Bishop of Liverpool. Here we see Dean Edward Patey, Dean of Liverpool, dropping in for a word with Bob. The Dean was a very exuberant character who brought all sides of religion together in the city.

Radio Merseyside started broadcasting on 22 November 1967, when at 12.30p.m. a Gerry Marsden jingle set England's third biggest BBC local radio station underway. There had been local BBC broadcasting in the area before this date. Liverpool had the call sign 6LV and had started on Wednesday 11 June 1924 with an official opening from the Philharmonic Hall. The station moved to its present site in Paradise Street from Commerce House in Sir Thomas Street in 1982. The official opening, seen here, was performed by Prince Charles.

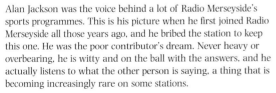

Alan Jackson was the voice behind a lot of Radio Merseyside's sports programmes. This is his picture when he first joined Radio Merseyside all those years ago, and he bribed the station to keep this one. He was the poor contributor's dream. Never heavy or overbearing, he is witty and on the ball with the answers, and he actually listens to what the other person is saying, a thing that is becoming increasingly rare on some stations.

Roger Phillips is one of those presenters who can handle a phone-in. He answers the queries and problems with intelligence. Another lad who has wandered around the stations a little, Roger has a brother called Gerry Phillips who is one of life's nice guys, looks like Roger but without the beard and a little more hair. He too has crossed the city, more than once.

Is this area down for the redevelopment that it needs? The view is from the Engineer's Monument over to the Dock Branch entrance of the Mersey Tunnel. It does seem a little under-used in this picture, doesn't it?

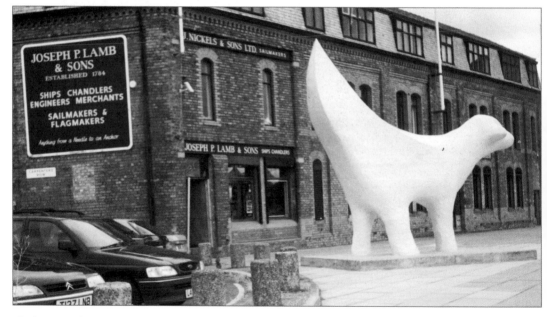

The banana-coloured lamb that appeared in Liverpool in 1998 and has titivated the city ever since. The graffiti it has attracted would make a book on its own and the lamb has been moved twice. It has now found a fitting home outside Joseph P. Lamb's shop outside the Albert Dock complex. I'm still looking for the concrete sheep dog that kept moving it.

And in the End . . .

The twentieth century changed Liverpool so much that a Rip Van Winkle would not recognise much of the city centre – the Town Hall, a few municipal buildings and St George's Hall perhaps, but little else. What will the twenty-first century bring to the city? The threat of war between this country and a neighbour seems remote. Will something happen to cause a rebuild in our city centre? All we can do is look at the place as it is today, and make a mental note that each one of us will try to do a little to make this place a better one. Better to live in, better to walk in, and nicer for the people sharing the streets, shops and buses with us.

The ferries are still with us and breathing welcome energy into the River Mersey. It's still a pleasant way to spend a Sunday afternoon, especially if you have youngsters to look after, sailing on the Heritage Cruise, whispering a chorus of 'Ferry 'Cross the Mersey' under your breath and wondering, what would happen if the boat didn't turn round and kept going to the other side of the world.

The Pier Head, 1999.

Renshaw Street. I expect it to be renamed Rapid Street any day now. It was at the top of Renshaw Street that the *Mersey Beat* newspaper started in 1961. Now that's something they should put a plaque up to.

Talking of plaques, what about our famous lady poetess, Felicia Hemans? Born in Duke Street in September 1793, as Felicia Dorothea Browne, she was famous for her moving poetry, and became a national figure. She wrote 'The Boy Stood on the Burning Deck' (Casablanca), 'Songs of Our Fathers' and many sea songs. Her house in Duke Street could do with a facelift and one of those blue plaques that we are told are going to be put on historic buildings and sites.

117

Prime sites in city centres have been snapped up and redeveloped. Colin's Bridewell (above) at the intersection of Campbell Street and Argyle Street, once a police station with prison cells, has been converted into a restaurant. Charles Roberts has long since ceased to use it as stabling for horses. This was the scene in 1999, and the picture on the left shows the buildings that then stood opposite.

The Beatles still continue to have an influence on Liverpool 30 years after moving on. Matthew Street, the Cavern and the Beatle shop still draw the tourists and make a pleasant nostalgic stroll for Liverpudlians. Here we have Arthur Dooley's sculpture entitled 'Mother Liverpool' though it looks more like 'Lady Madonna'. The words beneath are a pun on the book about the Russian Revolution: *Ten Days That Shook The World*, and you will notice there are only three dolls yet four initials on the wall. There was a fourth doll with wings at the side, representing Paul, but that has vanished. This tribute is well known and yet everybody owns it. The plaques either side were put up after the death of John Lennon, as was the doll with 'Lennon Lives' above it. The plaque below the doll has the first verse of 'Imagine' on it.

The Beatles Festival grows each year, and August 1999 saw a great weekend with bands and events all over the city. Ex-Beatle Pete Best reopened his club and *Yellow Submarine* was reissued as a highlight of the festival. Long may it continue to spread friendship and good feelings, and you can always nip round the corner for a chat with Eleanor Rigby (below).

Tommy Steele's 'contribution to the genius of the Beatles', and the people of Liverpool. Although it was cast in bronze, Tommy charged the city a mere 3p for the statue – or *Half a Sixpence*, the title of Tommy's hit show. It is said that just before the sack was dropped into the molten bronze a four-leaf clover was put in, for luck, a page from the Bible, for spiritual guidance, and a poem, for lovers. Nice one Tommy!

119

Above: There is one haven of peace and quiet that I really like in Liverpool's city centre. It's the garden behind the Blue Coat Chambers, off School Lane. The small but pleasant area is always awash with colour, statues and things seem to spring up constantly, and there is always a seat for a minute's quiet reflection. There is a book shop and heritage shop at the front and a café, too.

P.S. WE LOVE YOU. Yes I know I've altered one word but I would like to make one last point. If ever a man deserved recognition by his adopted home town that man is Joseph Williamson. 'The Mole of Edge Hill' did much to alleviate poverty in Liverpool. He gave away much of his fortune, which was considerable, anonymously and with little fuss. The more we know about him, and we are learning more every week, the more we see his kind and considerate nature. He was quickly and simply buried in 1840 in the Tate family vault in the graveyard of St Thomas' Church at the end of Paradise Street, on Park Lane corner. When the church was pulled down in 1905, all the bodies *except one* were moved. Yes you've guessed it – our Joseph. Why his was not moved is a mystery. The wits at the time said he was buried with a spade in his coffin so he'll have tunnelled his way out of there by now. So here he rests, under a parking space, roughly where 'X2' is marked, the man who was proud to be called 'A Liverpool Gentleman' and who did so much for the poor. Can't we do something for him?

Acknowledgements

Tony Hall and the *Liverpool Daily Post and Echo*; friend and author Ted Gray for his tram pictures; fellow historian Chris Makepeace for some photos from his collection; Gordon Coltas (Locofotos) for the use of his steam train pictures; Alan J. Gilbert for his photos of the Liverpool Overhead Railway; Ged McCann for his help with the older photographs; Colin Hunt, *Echo* librarian, for his help over the years; Alan Jackson, Radio Merseyside, for pleasant Sunday afternoons, Linda MacDermott, Billy Butler, Wally Scott and Billy Mahr for airtime given, and Liverpool for being there when I needed a friend.